Message of Bhagavad Gita

(In 126 Chosen Shlokas)

Part 3: ASI - You are THAT

Transcribed and Edited by Atmajyotis
(Based on Sri Prabhuji's Satsangs)

An offering from

LIGHT OF THE SELF FOUNDATION

Dedication

Many Atmajyotis have worked selflessly to transcribe
and publish this book based on talks of
Sadguru Sri Prabhuji.

With deep love and respect we dedicate this book to
all Atmajyotis. May this effort of all Atmajyotis reach
spiritual seekers all over the world, with this intention,
we release this book.

lokāha samasthāha sukhino bhavantu

Gita Jayanthi, December 2022

TABLE OF CONTENTS

FOREWORD

Srimad Bhagavad Gita is the sacred teaching of Sri Krishna. During the Mahabharata war, Arjuna's mind was full of anxiety and sorrow; he was confused between Dharma and Adharma. Bhagavad Gita is the teaching of Sri Krishna to the confused and depressed Arjuna. He was shown the path of Dharma by the supreme grace of the Lord.

Bhagavad Gita however isn't just a message delivered to Arjuna alone, it is the universal message given by the Vishwa Guru Sri Krishna to the entire human race. Arjuna was just an instrument. It is a sacred teaching for each and every one of us. What is the teaching? The Gita gives us the wisdom to attain liberation. It is a sacred scripture that shows us the path to *mukti* and uplifts us.

What do we have to do for that? ***ātmano mokshārtam jagad hitayacha*** - (Self Realization and Social Service) should be the mantra of our life. Hence the main teaching of Sri Krishna in Bhagavad Gita is *Brahma Vidya* (Knowledge of the Absolute) and *Yoga Shastra* (Yogic Science). Once we realize that the individual self and the supreme Self are one and the same, we attain *moksha*, we are liberated. Hence Sri Krishna teaches the truth of the inner self through Brahma Vidya, the knowledge that helps us merge with the supreme Self, Paramātma. To attain this knowledge, *brahmajnāna*, the mind should be purified. Hence Sri Krishna teaches us Yoga Shastra - how to lead an ethical and moral life and walk on the path of Dharma. This alone helps us to purify our minds.

yatra yogeśhvaraḥ kṛiṣhṇo
yatra pārtho dhanur-dharaḥ
tatra srir vijayo bhūtir
dhruvā nītir matir mama

Wherever there is Sri Krishna, the Lord of all Yoga, and wherever there is Arjuna, the supreme archer, there will also certainly be unending opulence, victory, prosperity, and righteousness. Of this, I am certain.

This sloka highlights the supreme importance of studying the Gita. Just like Arjuna, we should all become disciples of Sri Krishna. The teaching of Gita should be implemented in our day-to-day life. Only then 'Sri', meaning success in material life and 'Vijaya', meaning success in spiritual life will be obtained. This is the most important verse told by Sri Krishna in the last verse of the last chapter of the Bhagavad Gita (BG 18.78). The ones who study and implement Bhagavad Gita in their day-to-day life and teach this supreme knowledge to others are the closest and most lovable to God. Is there anything more important in life than being close to God?

Atmajyoti Satsang's Gita Jyoti Study Circles have many volunteers who are doing selfless service. The acharyas and acharyanis of the Study Circles are involved in various activities like teaching Bhagavad Gita verses, explaining their meaning, giving discourses, and generally spreading the message of the Gita to the world. They are an inspiration to many people. This seva is sure to bring a lot of good merit to all, because this activity is most lovable to God.

With the intention of passing the message of Bhagavad Gita in a simplified manner, 126 slokas from the 18 chapters have been carefully selected and summarized into a book. There are many Atmajyotis who have put in efforts to preserve my teachings and transcribe them into a book which is understandable to one and all. May the Supreme Lord bless them and their families. May their efforts be fruitful. May the light and wisdom of Gita flow into the lives of many more and uplift the entire world.

Sri Prabhuji
December 2022

PREFACE

The Bhagavad Gita is the song sung by the Lord. Listening to the Bhagavad Gita, chanting its verses and spreading the knowledge of Bhagavad Gita is considered very noble work.

Of all the *yajnas* and *pujas* that we offer to the Almighty, offering or spreading the wisdom of the scriptures is the greatest and noblest of all. All forms of worship give us good merit, but the greatest merit is gained by *jnāna yajna*, the service of spreading the Lord's message to the world.

Bhagavad Gita is a spiritual scripture. The path of spirituality shows us the divinity within. We look for God everywhere; we go to temples and undertake pilgrimage. But salvation lies only in realizing our own divinity. Bhagavad Gita is the Song of the Lord Himself, the ultimate truth imparted by Bhagavān Sri Krishna to Arjuna. Thus one who wishes to reach the ultimate reality has to necessarily study the Gita.

The Gita is the essence of all our scriptures - the Upanishads and the Vedas. Vedas are four in number - *rig, yajur, sāma and atharvana*. They begin with *karmakānda* and end with *jnānakānda*. In the *jnānakānda*, the portion which explains the meaning and essence of Vedas is called Upanishad.

Upanishad consists of the essence of all the Vedas. There are several Upanishads, 108 or even more. Out of these, the three great acharyas - Shankara, Madhva and Ramanuja have written the abstract or *bhashya* for ten important Upanishads.

The Upanishads contain the revelations of our ancient sages about the truth of existence - which is 'I am in the divine and the divine is in me'. The study of the Upanishads is also a *jnāna yajna*. The essence of the Upanishads is narrated by Sri Krishna to Arjuna in the Bhagavad Gita. Therefore if we study the Gita, the truth realized by the great rishis will be realized by us as well.

The realization of this Truth is called Jnāna. Jnāna destroys *ajnāna* - that about which we are ignorant. What is it that we do not know? We know everything about the outer world, like how to be a businessman, an engineer, how to cook etc. But what we do not know is, 'Who am I?' We assume that 'I' refers to the body, man or woman. We can go only as far as the body, mind and intellect and we think this is 'I'.

The Bhagavad Gita eliminates this ignorance about our identity with body, mind and intellect. It reveals that they are only the instruments or vehicles through which we operate!

Says Bhagavān, your mind, body and intellect are also vehicles, just as a car, bus or airplane is. You are the passenger, the *jivātma* who inhabits the body, mind and intellect. You are the Paramātma, the energy driving this vehicle. *mukti* or liberation is when you, the *jiva* realizes 'I am not this body, mind and intellect, I am one in the divine, I am *ātmaswaroopi*. So the essence of Bhagavad Gita is,

nānu, nānembudu nānalla
ee deha mana buddhi nānalla
sachchidānandātma shiva nānu nāne
shivoham shivoham shivoham

I am not what I think I am, I am not this body and mind or intellect; I am pure consciousness, Shivoham, Shivoham, Shivoham.

Over several lifetimes, we would've experienced a lot of good and bad things, accumulated merits and demerits. To experience and exhaust the results of these good-bad results, we have to be reborn yet again and again, *punarapi maranam, punarapi jananam, punarapi janani jatare shayanam*, sings Adi Shankaracharya; we are compelled to go through the repeated cycles of birth and death, and thus we end up in the mother's womb again and again.

With every new birth comes *ajnāna*, ignorance. With ignorance comes *pāpa-punya*, merit and demerit, which keep accumulating. This treasure-chest of endless *pāpa-punya* can be emptied only by diving into the *jnāna* of Bhagavad Gita.

"Can I let only the demerits go, and hang on to the merits?" is the clever question asked by the mind! But, says Krishna, both *pāpa-punya*, good-bad should go, because both are shackles that bind us. *pāpa* is the iron shackle and *punya* is the golden shackle, and we do not know which one binds us in what manner, both will certainly bind us to birth and death. Releasing ourselves from this bondage by realizing that "I am divine' is the message of Bhagavad Gita.

Right now, we operate in the world assuming, boasting that 'I am everything! There is no God! I am God!' The exact opposite of this is Self Realization - 'God is everything, There is nothing called I, I implies the ego'. When this realization happens, this is called *ātma jnāna, advaita jnāna.* We should study Bhagavad Gita for this *advaita jnāna*, the knowledge of liberation. There are 18 chapters in the Bhagavad Gita. It can be classified into three groups of six chapters each. In the first six chapters, the Lord explains who we are. In the next 6 chapters, He reveals about Himself, that is Ishwara, the creator. In the last six chapters, that is from 13th to 18th chapters, He explains about our relationship with God. Thus the Bhagavad Gita is the essence of the mahavākya of Upanishads - *tat tvam asi* - You Are That.

tat means 'Ishwara', **tvam** means 'you', **asi** means 'you are Ishwara', which means you are the form of Ishwara. We may feel "oh no, how is this possible? how can I be the form of God, this is not acceptable, this is thought is sin, this is injustice". This happens because we mistake the I for the Ego. When we stop identifying with the Ego, the real 'I' is revealed, we will realize 'I am Ishwara'. That is liberation, taught in the Bhagavad Gita.

ātma darshanam brahma darshanam
brahma darshanam satya darshanam

First and foremost we need to investigate, understand and become aware of what or who is this 'I'. This is called *ātma darshana*. Once we are aware about who we are, then the awareness of God will happen. This is called *brahma darshana*. Realizing that *ātma* and *brahma* are the same is *satya darshana*. This is the ultimate truth and everything else is a lie, a dream, an illusion - *māya*. The Bhagavad Gita leads us out of this illusion.

So, what is the subject matter of the Bhagavad Gita? Essentially, the Gita talks about two things - Jnāna (knowledge) and Karma (action). What kind of Jnāna? *ātmajnāna*; who am I, what is my relationship with God? What is Karma? How to lead life, how to perform action, how to purify my heart and attain liberation - this is called *karma mārga*, the Path of Karma. *ātmajnāna* implies *brahmajnāna*. Karma tells the way to lead our life. Understand these two and you will be liberated, says Lord Krishna.

No other scripture in the entire world teaches the means of liberation with such clarity and simplicity. The Gita has more than 700 verses. It might not be possible for most of us to study all the 700-plus verses; hence this effort of distilling the essence of the Bhagavad Gita in 126 selected verses. The summary of these 126 verses have been further divided into three parts and published as three separate books; hence we need to read all the three books to get the entire essence of the Gita.

This book has the summary of chapters 13 to 18, explained with the selected verses, and published as MESSAGE OF BHAGAVAD GITA Part 3: Asi - You Are THAT.

- Sri Prabhuji

CHAPTER 13: KṢHETRA KṢHETRAJÑA VIBHĀGA YOGA

Shloka 2

The Supreme Divine Lord said: O Arjuna, this body is termed as kṣhetra (the field of activities), and the one who knows this body is called kṣhetrajña (the knower of the field) by the sages who discern the truth about both

As we discussed earlier, the 18 chapters of Bhagavad Gita can be subdivided into sets of six each, based on their content and focus. This can easily be explained within the framework of the *mahavākya – tat tvam asi* or You are That. The first six chapters are about You or *tvam*, the next six are about Supreme Reality or *tat* and the last six are about the relationship between the two or *asi*.

Since we are now discussing the 13th chapter, we have come to the part of the Gita where Sri Krishna explains the relationship between the individual and the Self or *jivātma and paramātma*. Sri Krishna explains the difference between the known and the knower – *kshetra and kshetrajna*. We can understand this better through some examples.

The known and knower can also be thought of as the seen and seer. If there is a wall in front of me, the wall is the seen and I am the seer. So there is a duality between the seer and the seen or the knower and the known. We tend to focus all our attention on the object we see or know. We have to move from the seen to the seer, known to the knower. That is enlightenment. The knower is *kshetrajna*. The knower is God.

When I look at a photo, who is actually seeing it? Yes, my eyes are looking at the photo and my mind is seeing it through them. My intellect is seeing it through my mind and my ātma is seeing it through the intellect. So in this chain of eyes, mind, intellect and ātma, who is the real seer? ātma is the real seer because it is powering the eyes, mind and intellect which are its instruments. If they are not enlivened by consciousness, none of them can function. Also, ātma is the source of the entire chain. Since it is the Supreme Reality, we cannot go beyond it.

All the objects we can see are called the field of operation or *kshetra*. The one who is aware of the field of operation is called the *kshetrajna*. For instance, the body is *kshetra* and the *sakshi* or Consciousness who knows the body-mind–intellect is the *kshetrajna*. Consciousness is aware of physical sensations in the body, feelings and thoughts in the mind and ideas and decisions in the intellect. When we shift our focus from the known to the knower, we realize our oneness with God. In fact, when we say, "I see the wall," what we mean is that we are seeing the wall because we think we are the body-mind-intellect. We are identifying with the seeing apparatus instead of with the Seer. To move from the known to the knower, from the seen to the seer is our spiritual journey.

Why is Sri Krishna saying this? Because we are confusing ourselves with the body. I say "I am the body". Sri Krishna says you are not the body. You're the knower of the body, the knowing principle, Consciousness, which is different from the body. The body is the *kṣhetra*,field. *kṣhetra* comes from the Sanskrit word *kṣhēna*. It indicates that which has birth, growth and decay. That which becomes weak. kṣhēna means becoming weak. So the body is born, grows, becomes weak and dies. In that sense the body is *kṣhetra*.

Another meaning of body is field, an agricultural field where you sow seeds and reap fruits. If you sow mango seeds, a mango tree will grow. So the body is a field for experiencing Karma. If you do good Karma you will get good, favorable results in life. If you do bad Karma, you will experience unfavorable results or suffering in life. In that sense, the body is a field.

So the body is made up of matter, gross material. The knowing principle is Consciousness, which is not matter, not physical. Know the difference. You are really the knower, the Consciousness principle who knows the field called body. The body is different from you. So what do you have to know?

nānu nānembudu nānalla
ee deha, mana, buddhi nānalla
sachchidānandātma shiva nānu nāne
shivoham shivoham shivoham

Know that you are not the body, mind or intellect. The body, mind and intellect are matter, material. You are Pure Consciousness, *kṣhetra-jña*. So Sri Krishna says those who know the difference between *kṣhetra* and *kṣhetrajña* are wise men, Jnānis. Thus by knowing this difference, we also become wise.

sri-bhagavān uvācha,
idaṁ sharīraṁ kaunteya
kṣhetram ity abhidhīyate
etad yo vetti taṁ prāhuḥ
kṣhetra-jña iti tad-vidaḥ II 13.2 II

****

CHAPTER 14: GUNA TRAYA VIBHĀGA YOGA

Shloka 4

O' son of Kunti, for all species of life that are produced, the material nature is the womb, and I am the seed-giving Father

O' Arjuna, there are many living beings and different types of animals in this Universe. For them, nature is the mother and I am the father, says Sri Krishna.

Chapter 14 is called Guna Traya Vibhaga Yoga, *guna traya* meaning the three qualities of nature.

The three qualities of nature have to be understood. Why so? Because you are trapped in *maya, prakriti*. *māya* has three qualities: *sattva guna, rajo guna and tamo guna.* You are trapped in these three qualities of nature. So, if you're in jail and if you want to escape from it, you have to understand the jail itself. Likewise, *prakriti* has imprisoned you by these three qualities. You have to understand these three qualities to get out of her clutches and reach God, attain God.

sattva guna gives joy, *rajo guna* makes you active, and *tamo guna* makes you dull and sleepy. All of us are driven by these three qualities: joy, activity and dullness. You have to go beyond these three qualities. Ravana, Kumbakarana, Vibhishana represent these three qualities perfectly. Ravana represents *rajo guna* or hyper activity. Kumbhakarna represents *tamo guna* - dullness. He keeps on eating and sleeping. Vibhishana represents *sattva guna* or good qualities as he is always joyful and thinks of God.

Another example: A merchant was going through a forest when thieves captured him and tied him to a tree. After robbing him, one thief suggests that they kill him. The second thief prefers to bash him up badly so that he cannot escape. All three leave, but the third thief comes back, releases the merchant and helps him escape. The first guy who was ready to kill represents *tamo guna*. The second guy who stopped at killing but was willing to beat him is *rajo guna*. The third guy who released him and showed the way to escape is *sattva guna*. All are thieves, but *sattva guna* is a better thief, a better quality. *sattva guna* shows us the way of escape, the way of liberation, to reach God.

Now, the process is, from *tamo guna* or dullness, we have to move to *rajo guna* or activity. From *rajo guna* we have to move to *sattva guna* or peaceful qualities. Next we have to cross over *sattva guna* too to attain the Self, we have to go beyond all three qualities. This is the spiritual journey. That's why the Lord says "Understand that all living beings are born in *prakriti*". Body, mind and intellect are all prakriti, they come from nature. And the Consciousness comes from Bhagavān. So, in reality, you are actually a product of nature and Consciousness. You think that you have come from your father and mother, you trace yourself to your biological parents. Yes, the biological parents gave birth to you but really you belong to nature, prakriti. The body, mind, and intellect belong to nature and the Consciousness belongs to Bhagavān.

So, that means the real father is Consciousness and the real mother is Nature. Universal father and Universal mother are your real father and mother. That's what this shloka says:

tvam-eva mātā ca pitā tvam-eva
tvam-eva bandhush-ca sakhā tvam-eva
tvam-eva vidyā dravinam tvam-eva
tvam-eva sarvam mama deva deva

All relatives, friends and gurus, everybody is of the same nature. Finally, I have to trace back myself from the biological nature of relationship to the real Universal nature: Consciousness and Energy. This will help us to gradually understand that we are not bound to the earth but we can be free from the bondage of nature.

sarva-yoniṣhu kaunteya
mūrtayaḥ sambhavanti yāḥ
tāsāṁ brahma mahad yonir
ahaṁ bīja-pradaḥ pitā II 14.4 II

****

Shloka 26

Those who serve Me with unalloyed devotion rise above the three modes of material nature and come to the level of Brahman

Whatever you think, you become - this is a very powerful law of nature. You are creating yourself with your thoughts. A typical example used in Vedanta is the *bhramara-keeta nyāya*. *bhramara* is a type of insect. It catches another kind of insect, a *keeta*, in order to feed its larvae. It brings the live insect to its nest and leaves it there till its larvae get hungry. This insect is terrified that it will be killed by the *bhramara* any minute. So it constantly thinks of the *bhramara* in fear, awaiting its fate. The more the prey thinks of its predator, the more like the *bhramara* it becomes. Finally the *keeta* is transformed into a *bhramara*; it grows wings and flies away. Such is the power of thought.

Let's look at our own lives. What do we constantly think of? The husband thinks of his wife and the wife thinks of her husband. Or both of them think of money or the lack of it. So either they have plenty of money or very little of it. Instead of all this, if we think of God, we become one with him.

Do you have a photo that was taken at your wedding? You probably have another that was taken at your 25th or 50th wedding anniversary. Just keep them next to each other and take a look. In the wedding photo, you and your spouse look very different from each other. In the anniversary picture, both of you appear very alike indeed. Your faces have the same kind of creases, the same expressions, the same smiles. You have been thinking of each other for so many decades that you have begun to feel alike, think alike and look alike. Probably in your next life you will exchange your roles with each other, but still remain a couple. Yes, it happens because of the power of thought.

That is why Sri Krishna says, "If you serve me with pure devotion, and think of me constantly, you will transcend the three modes of *tamas, rajas* and *sattva* because you will become more and more like me. Ultimately you realize that you are one with me."

māṁ cha yo 'vyabhichāreṇa
bhakti-yogena sevate I
sa guṇān samatītyaitān
brahma-bhūyāya kalpate II 14.26 II

****

Shloka 27

I am the basis of the formless Brahman, the immortal and imperishable, of eternal dharma, and of unending divine bliss

In the earlier verse Lord said that you will reach Bhagavān or reach supreme reality if you constantly meditate on him. Now why should we meditate on him? Why should we reach him? That is the question, Why? Because he is *avyaya* - immutable. *amruta* - eternal, deathless. He is Dharma - he is the foundation of Dharma. He is the foundation of eternal Bliss. So if you want to attain eternal bliss, if you want to attain eternal Dharma, if you want to attain eternal life and if you want to attain something birthless and deathless then you have to constantly meditate on Bhagavān. Then you will reach Him.

brahmaṇo hi pratiṣhṭhāham
amṛitasyāvyayasya cha
śhāśhvatasya cha dharmasya
sukhasyaikāntikasya cha || 14.27 ||

****

CHAPTER 15: PURUSHOTTAMA YOGA

Shloka 1

The Supreme Divine Personality said: They speak of an eternal ashvattha tree with its roots above and branches below. Its leaves are the vedic hymns, and one who knows the secret of this tree is the knower of the Vedas.

The 15th chapter of the Bhagavad Gita is called Purushottama Yoga. Here Bhagavān describes different aspects of the Supreme Reality, of creation, of material nature, living beings, the world, vedic knowledge and also the relationship between them. So, you have to understand the total environment to understand the Supreme Reality - Purushottama. This is the purpose of the 15th chapter.

The first verse begins with a beautiful analogy of a tree; even more special is that it is an inverted tree. Normally the roots of the tree are in the ground and the shoots are in space. Whereas this inverted tree which God speaks of has the roots in the sky and the shoots are downwards.

What kind of tree is that?

The root represents the basis of existence. The basis of existence is above, meaning God, the supreme reality. In the entire creation the root is above, it represents the higher reality, Purushottama. God is the root of the entire creation. You cannot see the roots, but you can see the shoots and leaves. Similarly, you cannot see God but you can see the world that He has created. The basis of the entire creation (world) is God. The world is shown as an inverted tree. Here, the tree named *ashwattha* is mentioned, which is the Peepal tree. Why has He mentioned the Peepal tree specifically? That is because the Peepal tree perpetuates itself through its roots, which drop down from the branches and penetrate the ground. The Peepal tree also has a very long life span of 200-3000 years.

Likewise, the manifest world has a perpetual existence. Sri Krishna is not talking about eternal existence here. Eternal existence points to the Supreme Reality Purushottama. Perpetual existence means continued existence. In this context it is this tree, this world which goes on and on. It keeps on growing, keeps on continuing because of Karma, represented by the fruits and seeds of the tree. The fruits of Karma give rise to new Karma and it makes way for further life. The leaves of the tree represent the four vedas. They are the *rig veda, sāma veda, yajur veda, atharvana veda. veda* means knowledge, all kinds of knowledge, not just the four vedas; it includes science, mathematics, physics, medicine... All kinds of knowledge including spiritual knowledge are the leaves. Why is knowledge represented as leaves? Leaves prepare food with sunlight and water and feed the tree. Similarly, we use knowledge to act, to create something more. This leads to more actions, more results and more karmic impressions. This perpetual cycle will continue.

The beautiful picture of Sri Krishna as a baby sleeping on a Banyan leaf is an analogy that represents this concept... *vatasya patrasya pute shayānam*. Little Krishna, representing Purushottama or Supreme Reality, rests playfully on the (Banyan) leaf of vedic knowledge which floats on the causal waters. (after dissolution the world goes into causal form).

So, the Vedic knowledge or any knowledge will perpetuate the existence of the tree. Knowledge creates more action, more action in turn creates more knowledge; the tree keeps on growing. However, is it possible to cut the tree? Yes, it is possible to cut the tree by cutting the karmic impressions through Karma Yoga and Bhakti Yoga. This is how we can understand the analogy of a tree with roots above and branches below. It helps us understand the relationship between God and the world.

sri-Bhagavān uvācha
ūrdhva-mūlam adhaḥ-śhākham
aśhvatthaṁ prāhur avyayam I
chhandānsi yasya parṇāni
yas taṁ veda sa veda-vit II 15.1 II

****

Shloka 5

Those who are free from vanity and delusion, who have overcome the evil of attachment, who dwell constantly on the Self and on God, who are free from the desire to enjoy the senses, and are beyond the dualities of pleasure and pain, such liberated personalities attain My eternal Abode

In this verse Lord Krishna gives the qualities that are required to realize Him. *nirmāna-mohā* - to drop the ego and the attachment; *jita-saṅga-doṣhā* - to drop interest in the unnecessary things; *adhyātma-nityā* - contemplating on Bhagavān every day; *vinivṛitta-kāmāḥ* - dropping all desire-oriented actions *sukha-duḥkha-sanjñair* - going beyond happiness and unhappiness; *vimuktāḥ* - become free from these; *amūḍhāḥ* - the wise men; *tat avyayaṁ padam gachchhanty* - they will attain the supreme reality

What are these qualities? - First, we should drop all unnecessary actions. Unnecessary actions are that which are selfish in nature. We all have a lot of desires, and each of them propel us to do something. By dropping those desires which are unnecessary we can free our time and focus on what is really necessary. Else we will be running around doing a lot of petty things. We need to create time and space for God. Drop unnecessary desires.

Then what else could be done? One can go beyond happiness and unhappiness, beyond. It disturbs the mind, causes ripples in the mind. To reach God we have to make the mind calm and turn our attention inwards. The ego that says 'I am the doer, I am the so and so' should also be dropped. That ego has to be dropped. With ego one cannot attain Bhagavān . Dropping of the ego is a mandatory requirement. Next attachment to external things has to be released. Attachment binds us. Become free from the attachment to turn inward. These are the qualities required for realizing God.

And of course, that alone is not sufficient. We have to be *adhyātma-nityā* - constantly meditate on paramātma, the Supreme Reality. This is the process not just to attain the Lord, but to achieve anything in life. If somebody wants to become a doctor, he has to study for long hours, he has to prepare for entrance exams, he has to drop movies, cricket, TV etc and has to focus on his studies. He has to constantly think of medicine, of that subject without diverting his attention. If he says, no, I am addicted to watching TV, he has to drop that addiction too. The qualities that are required to reach God are the same qualities required to achieve success in life as well. They are not extraordinary. One needs to drop all unwanted things and focus. That's it.

nirmāna-mohā jita-saṅga-doṣhā l
adhyātma-nityā vinivṛitta-kāmāḥ ll
dvandvair vimuktāḥ sukha-duḥkha-sanjñair l
gachchhanty amūḍhāḥ padamavyayaṁ tat ll15.5 ll

****

Shloka 6

Neither the sun nor the moon, nor fire can illumine that Supreme Abode of Mine. Having gone there, one does not return to this material world again

God had told in earlier shlokas that you will attain His abode. What is His abode like?

na tad bhāsayate sūryah - there is no sun there; *na śhashāṅkah* - no moon, *na pāvakaḥ* - no fire. God says here that there is no sunlight, no moon light and no fire also in His abode. Why would anyone want to go to such a place? Isn't it? *yad gatvā na nivartante* - after reaching that place, one does not come back. *tad dhāma paramaṁ mama* - that is My supreme abode, says Sri Krishna.

The sun, the moon, the fire are all part of material nature. They are all part of the matter, *prakriti*. But God is Purushottama; the Supreme Consciousness. *prakriti* is dependent on Purushottama. Nature has no independent reality. Consciousness is an independent reality. It is Consciousness that creates the sun, moon and fire, but Consciousness itself is free from sun, moon and water.

When electricity passes the tube light will glow, the bulb will glow, the fan will rotate. Electricity exists and is independent of the tube light or bulb or fan. Electricity is 'the cause' for the operation of the appliances. Tube light, bulb and fan are the relative 'effect'.

Likewise, the Supreme Consciousness says that there is no sun, there is no moon and there is no fire in Me because I am the 'Source'. I'm the source of the sun, moon and water. Sun, moon and fire are all perishable. They all have death. After a few billion years the sun will die. You don't have to worry about the sun's death as your life span is only a hundred years. So, why do you depend on material nature for your life? Consciousness is the source of material nature and that is eternal. You can go back to Consciousness. This is the teaching.

na tad bhāsayate sūryo
na śaśhāṅko na pāvakaḥ I
yad gatvā na nivartante
tad dhāma paramaṁ mama II 15.6 II

****

Shloka 7

All living beings in this material world are My eternal parts. But bound by material nature, they are struggling with the six senses including the mind

The scriptures say that there are 8.4 million species of living organisms on earth. This includes micro-organisms like bacteria and macro-organisms like the elephant. Though this encompasses a huge bandwidth of forms, the consciousness in all living beings is the same. This enlivening consciousness is God. That is why Sri Krishna says, "I am in all beings and they are in me." So all life is sacred.

To create a living organism, Consciousness - *purusha* takes a part from Nature - *prakriti*. Our mind and sense organs come from Nature. Consciousness then enlivens the mind and sense organs, identifies with them and says, "I am an individual - *jiva*. I am a separate entity. The world and God are different from me." Though this identification is false, we believe it to be true. This mistaken belief traps in a tug of war with our mind and sense organs. When we drop the belief I am the body, mind and intellect, we realize that we were always one with the Lord.

mamaivānśho jīva-loke
jīva-bhūtaḥ sanātanaḥ I
manaḥ-ṣhaṣhṭhānīndriyāṇi
prakṛiti-sthāni karṣhati II 15.7 II

****

Shloka 15

I am seated in everyone's heart, and from Me come remembrance, knowledge and forgetfulness. By all the Vedas am I to be known; indeed, I am the compiler of Vedanta, and I am the knower of the Vedas

sarvasya chāhaṁ hṛidi sanniviṣhṭo – I am in the heart of all living beings. The *smriti* or 'memory' and Jnāna or 'knowledge' both are because of my presence. I am the cause of the memory and knowledge and am also the remover of the same.

I am the source of all vedas. All vedas teach about me. The end of veda is called Vedanta. Vedanta gives the knowledge of Bhagavān . I am the source of Veda and I am the creator of Vedanta too.

God is telling about his glory; for us to understand. First, he says that he is present in the hearts of all living beings. Be it an ant, be it an elephant, be it a tiger or be it a monkey or be it a rat or a human being, God is present in the heart of all living beings as Consciousness. Now, it's not that ant has less of Godliness and human beings have more of Godliness. God or Consciousness is the same in all living beings.

Living beings have something called memory and something called knowledge. The knowledge and memory are not because of body and mind, but because of consciousness. Consciousness illuminates both the body and the mind, then we get memory and knowledge. Electricity passes through the tube light and then the light glows; light is caused by the electricity, but electricity itself is not light. Similarly, the presence of the consciousness creates knowledge and memory in the living being.

And, to know God, what is the source? The vedas are the source of knowledge about God. Now, vedas also have come from God only. Without vedas coming from God, you cannot know about God. Vedanta is the science, with Upanishads, teachings of realized masters which in turn come from none other than Bhagavān. That's why they are authentic. Otherwise, anything else becomes a product of the human mind, a fiction that is not authentic. What comes from God's mind is authentic, it is Vedanta.

sarvasya chāhaṁ hṛidi sanniviṣhṭo I
mattaḥ smṛitir jñānam apohanaṁ cha II
vedaiśh cha sarvair aham eva vedyo I
vedānta-kṛid veda-vid eva chāham II 15.15 II

****

Shloka 19

Those who know Me without doubt as the Supreme Divine Personality truly have complete knowledge. O Arjuna, they worship Me with their whole being

O' Arjuna, one who is not deluded by the nature of prakriti, the nature of māya, one who is wise enough... he knows the Purushottama- the Supreme

Lord, and he constantly remembers Me and worships Me.

In the earlier shloka Sri Krishna said that all living beings are a part of Himself or Consciousness. Then this Consciousness gets deluded by māya, gets confused, and identifies with the body and mind, sense organs and sense objects. It forgets its true nature as Purushottama or the Supreme Lord. The wise are not deluded, they are not confused by the 'seen". They go back to the 'seer', Consciousness, and constantly worship Him. And eternally, always think of Him and worship Him. They go back to the Lord.

yo mām evam asammūḍho
jānāti puruṣhottamam I
sa sarva-vid bhajati māṁ
sarva-bhāvena bhārata II 15.19 II

****

CHAPTER 16:
DAIVĀSURA SAMPAD VIBHĀGA YOGA

Shloka 1

The Supreme Divine Personality said: O scion of Bharata, these are the saintly virtues of those endowed with a divine nature—fearlessness, purity of mind, steadfastness in spiritual knowledge, charity, control of the senses, sacrifice, study of the sacred books, austerity, and straightforwardness

Chapter 16 is about divine and demoniac qualities. In the first verse Sri Krishna tells abouts the divine qualities one has to develop. Why should one develop divine qualities? These divine qualities help you to realize the Self. These are the requirements, prerequisites. For everything in life there is a prerequisite. If you have to go to college, high school is a prerequisite. If you have to go to science, basic science is a requirement. Similarly for Self knowledge, some divine qualities are the requirement, they are called *daivi sampath*. If you want to grow something in an agricultural field, the soil should be fertile. There should be water, there should be fertilizer, there should be sunlight, then only plants will grow. Similarly knowledge, Self knowledge will grow in a person who has the divine qualities. So that is why *daivi sampath* is important.

abhayam - Fearlessness. What is fearlessness? Someone is fearless when he has self confidence. Self confidence comes with faith in oneself. Faith in oneself comes when you have faith in the Guru and faith in the scriptures - veda māta. What does she say - she says *tat tvam asi,* she gives *atmajnāna*, Self knowledge. When you have *shraddha* - faith in the teaching of the Guru and the *shāstra*, together they give you self confidence. "Yes I am going in the right path of Self knowledge. I am in the right direction". Then there's no fear. That's called *abhayam.*

sattva samsuddhih - purity of the mind. The mind is your friend as well as the enemy. A disturbed mind is an enemy. A pure mind which is silent, which is helpful, which is cheerful, which is joyful, which doesn't have negative thoughts, which is full of positive thoughts and creativity is our friend - *satva samsuddhih* - is a friend.

jñāna-yoga-vyavasthitiḥ - therefore, focus on Jnāna Yoga. An engineering student says "I am in the path of engineering. I will study engineering well". A medical student says "I am a medical student, I'll study medicine well". Similarly, a person in Jnāna Yoga says "I'm on the path of Jnāna Yoga. Let me be fully involved in Jnāna Yoga". That commitment is *jñāna-yoga-vyavasthitiḥ*.

dānam - ability to give charity. Why should we give charity? Human beings by nature are greedy. "I want more, I want more". There's no satisfaction at all. So somewhere we should learn how to give. In the process, we will try to compensate for our greedy nature. We will develop compassion, ability to give. That's called *dāna*.

damah - my control over the sense organs. Our sense organs - eyes, ears, nose, tongue, touch - are attracted by many things. And these attractions can lead us to many trappings. A fish gets trapped by an insect tied to the hook of the fisherman and loses its life. The tongue, the taste of the tongue, causes the death of the fish. The deer gets attracted by the music of a hunter, then dies. Human beings can get attracted by any of the five sense organs. We should have control over the sense organs. What I should take and what I should not take. What is good for me? That's called *dama*.

yajnah - we have to develop a service attitude in life. I have to offer my services to the living beings, because God is everywhere in all forms of living beings. That's why offering our gratitude and service to the Lord in the form of the universe is called *Yajna*.

deva yajna, pitr yajna, manushya yajna, bhuta yajna, rishi yajna are the five types of Yajnas we have to perform everyday.

svādhyāya - study of the scriptures. It also means self awareness. I should not depend on somebody else telling me - about me. I should be aware of my qualities. Where do I need to improve? I have to be aware of that myself. I should live in awareness. Also, I should study the scriptures - the Vedas and Upanishads. This is called *svādhyāya*.

tapah - means penance or austerities. What kind of penance? Physical and mental penance. It is about taking control of ourselves, and working towards it by putting down rules and drawing limits on our habits. For example "I will have just one meal a day" is a penance. Or "I will take up this ritual" is penance. The reason why this penance is needed is that we face hardships and pleasures in life again and again, and we need the strength to face those hardships. The one who undertakes auterities is in control, has power, because he has voluntarily undertaken it. Then nothing will shake him from his inner peace.

jnana-yoga-vyavasthitih - commitment to Jnāna comes from commitment to *shravana, manana, nidhidhyāsa.* This is called *ātmano mokshartham.*

Yajna - service, is for *jagad-hita*. *ātmano mokshārtham, jagad hitāyacha* should be our way of life. *svādhyāya* is self-study as part of Jnāna Yoga.

ārjavam - straight-forwardedness. No crookedness. Inside and outside - one reality; not telling lies, being a simple, straight forward person. This makes the mind peaceful.

These are *daivi sampath* - divine qualities. Sri Krishna says these qualities are very important for Self Realization.

sri-bhagavān uvācha,
abhayaṁ satva-sanśhuddhir
jñāna-yoga-vyavasthitiḥ I
dānaṁ damaśh cha yajñaśh cha
svādhyāyas tapa ārjavam II 16.1 II

****

Shloka 2

(These are the saintly virtues of those endowed with a divine nature) - non-violence, truthfulness, absence of anger, renunciation, peacefulness, restraint from fault-finding, compassion toward all living beings, absence of covetousness, gentleness, shame, and lack of fickleness

Sri Krishna continues to describe the saintly qualities of evolved beings. Next he extols non-violence or ahimsa. What is non-violence? When we abstain from hurting others in order to achieve selfish goals, it is called non-violence. However, if someone tries to hurt us, we can defend ourselves. This does not violate the path of non-violence or **ahimsa**.

satyam or being truthful is another saintly quality. We have heard of the saying Honesty is the Best Policy. So we know that we have to tell the truth. But there are also parameters about how we should do it. We should be able to phrase it in such a way that it does not hurt anyone. The purpose of telling the truth is to correct the situation and not to offend others. The person to whom we speak should get authentic feedback from us and it should motivate him to change himself. It should not disturb him but result in meaningful, positive action.

Mastery over anger or **akrodah** is important. How can you control anger? Anger has two components – emotion and action. Usually anger makes us reactive because it triggers pain in us. In fact, psychological pain is called anger. We have no control over emotion, anger may also arise in us. What we can control is whether we act or react. If we react, we may shout or hurt someone. Our reaction may worsen the situation instead of improving it. The pain called anger can also be converted to meaningful, creative action. Mahatma Gandhi was thrown out of the train in Africa. The Apartheid system that existed there at that time did not allow people with dark skin to ride in the same carriage as those with white skin. He was very angry at being treated in this way, but he channelized this anger into the freedom struggle instead of raving and ranting uselessly.

tyāga means dropping the thought that I am the body, mind and intellect and understanding that I am pure consciousness.

As situations change the mind oscillates too. Favorable circumstances make us happy while unfavorable ones depress us. When we remain calm under all circumstances, maintaining equanimity, we achieve peace or ***shānthi***.

It is easy to find fault and judge others but this may not be a very helpful attitude. Unless this generates solutions, others may find this irritating too. If this is our habitual behaviour, friends may run away as soon as they see us coming! So we should be a part of the solution, never the problem. Not indulging in constant fault finding is ***apaiśhunam***.

daya is having compassion for all living beings. When we are able to cognise the Self in everyone, we will never hurt them. How can we see the Self in all beings? When someone hits me I feel pain. When an animal is injured, it also experiences pain. My pain is the same as the animal's pain. My friend's pain is the same as mine. Though outer forms are different, everyone experiences the same pain when they are hurt. Similarly though we appear different from each other, we experience the same happiness when things go well for us. When we understand this we see the Self in all beings and *daya* or compassion overflows from us.

maya makes this world look very attractive to us. So we develop an attachment to many things. Possessing something makes us happy while losing it fills us with sorrow. Not getting attached to anything is called *aloluptvaṁ*.

mardavaṁ is gentleness. When our discrimination is sharp, we realise that gentleness is the key. Our thoughts, words and deeds should be gentle. Even when we are firm, we can still be gentle. A judge may give a criminal a harsh sentence, but he phrases it gently. Our action should be appropriate, but gentle. That is *mardavaṁ*.

hri indicates shame. We should be ashamed of performing adharmic acts. This will help us to avoid flouting *dharma*. But we are often worried about what people will think of us even when we want to do dharmic acts. *hri* means being ashamed of doing the wrong thing but never shirking the responsibility of doing the right thing.

All of us have experienced how restless the mind can be. It flits from one topic to another, never settling anywhere. This can be compared to digging a well. If the person digging the well gets restless after digging ten feet and thinks, "I still did not hit water here. Let me try in a different place." If he changes his mind ten times, he will have ten dry pits which are useless to him. Instead if he had dug a hundred feet in one place he would have surely hit water. A person who has a restless mind will never achieve anything in life because he is constantly distracted from his goals. Even to get Self Knowledge, focus is crucial. *achāpalam* is having a focussed mind that is free from restlessness.

ahinsā satyam akrodhas
tyāgaḥ śhāntir apaiśhunam I
dayā bhūteṣhv aloluptvaṁ
mārdavaṁ hrīr achāpalam II 16.2 II

****

Shloka 3

(These are the saintly virtues of those endowed with a divine nature -) Smartness, forgiveness, fortitude, cleanliness, bearing enmity towards none, and absence of vanity

In continuation, of the many subtle virtues, Sri Krishna highlights *tejah* or smartness. An evolved person cannot say, "I am simple. I am divine. People can cheat me easily because I do not doubt anyone." No. We have to be smart as well as good. It is wonderful that we don't cheat anyone. However, we should also be smart enough not to let others cheat us. Yes, we don't hurt others, but we should be able to protect ourselves so that they don't hurt us.

There is a good story to illustrate this. When Bhagavān Buddha was walking in the forest, he heard of a poisonous snake that was biting and killing many people. He went to the snake and said, "O Snake please stop biting people." The snake agreed. The next time Bhagavān Buddha came that way, he saw that the snake had become very weak. When he asked the snake why he looked so thin, he said, "It is all because of you. You asked me not to bite anyone. Now that everyone knows that I won't harm them they hit me with sticks and pelt me with stones. They derive sadistic pleasure from torturing me. So I dare not go out of my hole to hunt for food. Following your advice has brought me to a very bad place in life." So Bhagavān Buddha said, "You are a foolish snake. Yes, I told you not to bite anyone. Did I tell you not to hiss at them? Hiss all you like. Pretend to be angry. Protect yourself but don't bite them." This is *tejah* or being smart enough not to get exploited, cheated or hurt.

Then Sri Krishna goes on to talk about **kshama** or patience. In the previous shloka he told us about *akrodah* or converting anger into meaningful action. There, anger arises and is then channelized. But if we have *kshama* there is no anger at all. Patience does not allow anger to sprout. What is the root of anger? Disappointment. When something doesn't happen according to my wishes, I'm disappointed and from this rises anger. If we are able to accept what is happening, then there is no anger. There is a well known prayer that says, "God, grant me the serenity to accept the things I cannot change, the courage to change the things I can, and the wisdom to know the difference." When we accept life as it comes, we act instead of reacting. We may try several things to resolve the situation. If they work, we accept it readily. If they don't, we accept that too. In neither case is there any anger. This is *kshama*.

However, at times perseverance can work miracles. Some have the ability to work undeterred by obstacles. Let's say that we are driving to a destination in our car. The road may be full of potholes and road humps. There may be traffic jams and detours, but we keep driving till we reach our destination. This is called **dhriti**. On the spiritual path, our destination is Self realization. We need to have a lot of perseverance and determination to reach this goal.

shaucham is external and internal purity. Keeping our body and surroundings clean is outer purity. Keeping the mind free from the wrong kind of thoughts is internal purity.

In the previous shloka we learnt about ahimsa or non-violence. But **adroha** is subtler than that. In non-violence, thoughts of violence may arise in the mind, but we don't execute them because we want to follow *ahimsa*. When we are furious with someone we may think, "I want to kill him." But we don't actually do it. However, in *adroha* such violent or hurtful thoughts never arise. There is only goodwill towards all. *adroha* means absence of ill will.

nāti-mānitā is humility. There are two kinds of people – those who think they know everything but actually don't and those who are aware that they know nothing. If we want to learn from those who know, we must have humility. If we think that we know everything, we can never learn. We have seen that water flows from a higher level to a lower level. Knowledge too flows from those who know to those who don't. But for this to happen, we have to be receptive. *nāti-mānita* means we understand that we are at a lower level so far as knowledge is concerned. So we are ready to receive it. When we surrender to the Guru in this way, knowledge flows to us.

Sri Krishna says that these are some of the qualities that make us eligible for Self Knowledge.

tejaḥ kṣhamā dhṛitiḥ
śhaucham adroho nāti-mānita I
bhavanti sampadaṁ daivīm
abhijātasya bhārata II 16.3 II

****

Shloka 4

O Partha, the qualities of those who possess a demoniac nature are hypocrisy, arrogance, conceit, anger, harshness, and ignorance

In this *daivāsura sampad vibhāga yoga*, after describing the divine qualities, Bhagavān, as a contrast, gives the demoniac qualities.

dambha means show-off, showing-off; *darpa* - that's pride; *abhimāna* - ego, *krodha* - anger, *pāruṣhya* - harsh words, *ajñāna* - ignorance. All these are asuri *sampath* or demonic qualities. Demoniac qualities lead to the downfall of a person. They cause damage to oneself as well as people around who interact.

dambha (show-off) - a person of a demoniac quality wants to do (various actions) because he has a lot of inferiority complex inside. So he wants to show-off. He covers it with external makeup. Because he feels inferior inside, he starts showing-off.

Then, **darpa** (pride). Pride of possession. I have this; I have that; all these are pride. God loves you for what you are, not for what you have, but a demoniac person doesn't understand inner qualities. Instead of that he is more interested in showing off the external things. He is more interested in accumulating.

Then, **abhimana** (ego). Ego is a feeling of I am body; I am mind; I am intellect. So, with this ego what will happen? You feel proud of your body, you feel proud of your mind. So, you believe you are a body and mind which takes you away from God. You identify with the physical structure.

krodhaḥ is anger. We have already seen in the earlier slokas about anger. Anger is because of desire. When there is anger, the person will use harsh words. Harsh words can hurt others.

And of course, coupled to all this is ***ajnāna*** (ignorance); ignorance of Self; ignorance of God; ignorance of the world. All these complicate the problem further.

So, these are the demoniac qualities. A person with demoniac qualities has a downfall in spiritual life. That is the purpose of Bhagavān, to outline divine and demonic qualities. Further demonic qualities are told in the next few slokas.

dambho darpo 'bhimānaśh cha
krodhaḥ pāruṣhyam eva cha I
ajñānaṁ chābhijātasya pārtha
sampadam āsurīm II 16.4 II

****

CHAPTER 17: SHRADDHĀ TRAYA VIBHĀGA YOGA

Shloka 2

The Supreme Lord said, according to the modes of nature acquired by the embodied soul, one's faith can be of three kinds- in goodness, in passion or in ignorance. Now hear about these

This chapter is called Shraddhā Traya Vibhāga Yoga.

shraddhā means faith. The faith is of three types - *sattvic, rajasic and tamasic*. Sri Bhagavān describes them here. Why is this description given? Because Arjuna asks Krishna - there are people who don't understand scriptures but they worship God with faith. They just have faith in God. What about them? To answer his question, Bhagavān responds thus.

In the Ramayana, we come across three different characters - Ravana, Kumbakarna and Vibhishana. Ravana's nature is very aggressive. He wants to achieve, he is an achiever. His faith is *rajasic* in nature. He undertakes severe penance for Lord Shiva, but no matter how much he tries, Shiva does not materialize in front of him. So, he goes on to shake Mount Kailasa itself - after which Shiva comes hurriedly to grant him a boon! This is an example of a *rajasic* faith, in which you can force even God to appear in front of you. This person will take a long time to develop inner qualities.

Whereas his brother Vibhishana represents *sattvic* nature. Although Vibhishana was born in a demonic family, he had all divine qualities. He did not see Rāma as an enemy but as a divine being, incarnation. He worshiped Rāma constantly, and thus Rāma made him his friend.

Look at the contrast between Vibhishana and Ravana. Ravana forced Shiva to appear in front of him. Whereas Vibhishana's nature made Rama take Vibhishana as his friend. This displays the *sattvic* quality.

Whereas the third brother Kumbakarna would just eat and sleep all the time. His nature is *tamasic*. When he meditated upon Brahmaji, Kumbakarna offered his own head as an offering to Brahmaji. This displays the qualities of *tamasic* type of faith.

In this chapter Sri Krishna goes on to further elaborate on *sattvic, rajasic* and *tamasic* qualities.

sri-bhagavān uvācha
tri-vidhā bhavati śhraddhā
dehināṁ sā svabhāva-jā I
sāttvikī rājasī chaiva
tāmasī cheti tāṁ Sriṇu II 17.2 II

****

Shloka 23

The words 'Om Tat Sat' have been declared as symbolic representations of the Supreme Absolute Truth, from the beginning of creation. From them came the brahmanas (realized/evolved beings), vedas (highest knowledge), and yajnas (selfless offering - way of life)

In this verse Sri Krishna tells about the importance of the mantra *Om tat sat.* om tat sat is a holy mantra, holy name.

When Brahmaji started creation, the first syllable he uttered was Om. What is the meaning of Om? Om itself is a holy word. Om, Om, Om … say it three times with eyes closed… Om itself has sound and silence. The sound of *omkāra* represents manifest reality. The silence of *omkāra* represents the unmanifest. Creation and unmanifest creation is represented by *omkāra. akāra, ukāra and makāra* (audible syllables of *omkāra*) represent the waking, dream and deep sleep states. Silence represents *turiya,* beyond waking, dream and deep sleep states. So in that sense *omkāra* is a total representation of reality, a complete representation of the manifest and unmanifest.

omkāra is a holy name. So Brahma first uttered the syllable Om - the sacred name which involves *saguna and nirguna* (God with attributes and without attributes), *sākara and nirākāra* (God with form and formless), total reality.

Then he uttered *tat sat*. Here *tat* means 'That'. What is 'That'? Brahman. That which is not available to your sense organs or mind is called *tat*. The absolute reality or Parabrahma is not available to your sense organs, hence the statement *tat tvam asi*. In *tat tvam asi, tvam* is *jiva* - the individual soul, which is available to you, you know. *tat* is what you don't know, what is not available to your sense organs and mind.

So *omkāra* is the totality and *tat* is beyond the sense organs and the mind. So Brahmaji is speaking of Parabrahma Narayana here. Brahmaji is remembering Supreme reality Parabrahma Narayana through *tat*. *omkāra* includes everything. *tat* is only specific to Parabrahma.

Next he remembers the nature of that *sat*, which is pure existence. This is also Parabrahma beyond the intellect, mind and sense organs. So does it mean there is nothing at all - *shunya*? Not at all. *sat* is 'existence', not 'non-existence'. It is not *asat*. So what exists beyond the sense organs and the mind is pure existence Parabrahma. When you see anything in the world, the tree is, the river is, the sun is, 'is' ness is referring to existence, it doesn't change, it cannot be seen either. Existence cannot be seen. Existence appears as a tree, appears as sun, appears as moon. Appearance can be seen, what is reality cannot be seen. That is called *sat*. That sat is pure Brahman. In one syllable so much is told.

So Brahmaji spoke these holy words *om tat sat*. This mantra is chanted at the beginning of any Yajna or holy ritual or any important activity. *om tat sat* purifies that activity. Just because Brahmaji first uttered these words, should I also use it? Why not? Don't we say 'Hello' when we make a phone call? Why do you use the word Hello? Graham Bell, the person who discovered the phone, used 'Hello' as the first word over the phone. Hello was his girlfriend's name! Now, all of us also call and say 'Hello' and follow the first person who said that.

brāhmaṇās tena vedāsh cha yajñāsh cha - with these words Brahmaji created Brāhmana. Brāhmana refers to all human beings. *vedāh* - then he gave us the Vedas. scriptures which tell us how to live our lives so that we are in tune with the universe. *yajñāsh cha* - then the way of living life as a service. So Brahmaji created the world with *om tat sat,* he created human beings, and he gave them how to lead life in the form of vedas and he told them your life should be in accordance with Yajna, service, *jagad hitāya*. So all these three things he did. That is why whenever we use the word om tat sat we are in tune with the universe. So Sri Krishna says even if somebody does *rajasic* and/or *tamasic* acts, which are not pure and *sattvic*, if they chant *om tat sat* their mind gets purified, their mind starts moving towards *sattvic* nature. This is the importance of the mantra *om tat sat*.

oṁ tat sad iti nirdeśho
brahmaṇas tri-vidhaḥ smṛitaḥ I
brāhmaṇās tena vedāsh cha
yajñāsh cha vihitāḥ purā II 17.23 II

****

Shloka 27

Being established in the performance of sacrifice, penance, and charity, is also described by the word Sat. And so any act for such purposes is named Sat

We already understood that sat means pure existence or Parabrahma. It is beyond the sense organs and mind. In this verse Sri Krishna gives us another meaning for the word *sat*. He says that any action that purifies us is called *sat karma*. We know that service activities like Yajna or sacrifice, *tapas* or austerities and *dāna* or charity are prescribed by the scriptures.

We have five types of Yajnas or sacrifices. They are called *pancha-mahā-yajna*. Revering our ancestors and helping senior citizens is called *pitru yajna*. Offering worship to the gods in various ways is *deva yajna*. Service to fellow human beings is *manushya yajna*. Showing compassion to animals is *bhuta yajna*. Understanding and sharing the teachings of the sages and scriptures is *rishi yajna*.

Performing *yajna* is very important because Lord Brahma himself has said that they help alleviate suffering in life. This can be compared to the prescription of a doctor. He tells us to take a vaccine to prevent some disease from attacking us. If we don't follow his recommendation, we will suffer if we fall sick. In the same way Yajnas protect us by keeping us on the path of Dharma, so that we don't accumulate negative Karma. When we don't engage in Yajna, we are prone to generate negative Karma that causes a lot of suffering.

Our miseries arise because we don't perform Yajna and *tapas*. **tapas** means following various types of self-discipline. A student who wants to score good marks in IIT studies for many hours every day. Till his exams are over he may postpone watching movies or going out with friends. This focussed studying helps him to score well in the exams. In spiritual life also we impose some discipline on ourselves. We may get up at 4 am to meditate or eat two meals a day instead of three. Introducing an element of discipline into our lives increases our focus towards the spiritual goal.

tapas also enhances our ability to face challenges in life. For instance the famous Indian athlete PT Usha practiced running on the seashore carrying a sandbag on her shoulders. This strengthened her muscles so much that she won many gold medals in prestigious competitions. When you overcome tough situations, you effortlessly breeze through easier ones. If you are used to sleeping on the floor, you will not complain when a mattress is unavailable. So we should deliberately focus on empowering ourselves through self-discipline or *tapas* to overcome the challenges life throws at us.

We understood the importance of yajna and tapas. What about **dāna** or charity? Charity helps to reduce our greed. We want more and more because we are never satisfied with what we have. Yajna is a way of life, *tapas* builds inner strength and *dāna* nurtures our satisfaction and compassion. These three together are called *sat* or sat karma. Living according to the teachings of God or Lord Brahma is *sat karma*.

All the actions that we perform to please God are also *sat karma*. It is considered as service to him. These actions don't have to be big, impressive ones. Even small, unimportant actions are recognised by God. We see an instance of this in the famous epic Ramayana. When the monkeys in the army of Lord Rama are carrying huge rocks to build a bridge across the ocean, a small squirrel also wants to help. Since his tiny paws cannot carry stones, he comes up with a smart idea. After wetting himself in the water, he rolls over dry sand which sticks to his fur. He then goes to the bridge under construction and shakes himself vigorously to drop the sand particles there.   Seeing the devotion of the squirrel, Lord Rama is moved. He strokes its back with love. It is

said that this resulted on the three white lines seen on
the back of every Indian squirrel.

So, even the smallest task that we perform as an
offering to God is *sat karma*. It is our intention and
devotion that count, not the importance of the task.

yajñe tapasi dāne cha
sthitiḥ sad iti chochyate I
karma chaiva tad-arthīyaṁ
sad ity evābhidhīyate II 17.27 II

****

CHAPTER 18: MOKSHA SANYĀSA YOGA

Summary

The 2nd and 18th chapters of the Bhagavad Gita are big ones. While the 2nd chapter on Sānkhya Yoga gives an introduction to all the teachings in the Gita, the 18th Chapter on Moksha Sanyāsa Yoga provides a summary at the end. As you are now aware, sanyāsa refers to renunciation and *moksha* to liberation. As the name *moksha sanyāsa yoga* suggests Chapter 18 deals with liberation through renunciation.

After listening to Sri Krishna's teachings, Arjuna is in a dilemma. He asks, "To attain liberation, what should I do? Should I renounce all my duties and responsibilities and become a monk? Should I run away from this battlefield? Tell me, Krishna, what is the difference between *sanyāsa* and *tyāga*?"

Let us understand whether there is any difference. A Sanyasi is a monk who has renounced the world. A *tyāgi* continues to fulfill his household responsibilities while focussing on the goal of Self Realization. Both of them strive for *moksha* in their own way. A monk doesn't have to work for his living because he can beg for food. He can devote most of his time to *shravana, manana and nidhidhyāsa* – listening to Vedantic truths, contemplation and meditation. He has no other obligations to fulfill. He is not required to perform rituals. His only duty is to share his wisdom with society.

A *tyāgi* has many responsibilities as a householder. He has to earn his living and take care of his family. He also has to support those who are in the stages of *brahmacharya, vānaprasta and sanyāsa* – students, senior citizens and monks. He has to perform the *pancha mahā yajnas* – offer worship to the Gods and ancestors, help fellow human beings, nurture animals and share the wisdom of the sages.

However, Sri Krishna tells Arjuna that *sanyāsa* and *tyāga* are not different. While a monk renounces his house and family physically, a *tyāgi* drops his attachment to the fruits of action. He continues to perform all tasks perfectly but mentally renounces his right to the results – *karmanyeva adhikāraste māphaleshu kadāchana.* He accepts both favorable and unfavorable outcomes as the grace of God. When we give up our attachment to results, our mind becomes calm. We remain equipoised saying, "God you have given me the fruit that I deserve according to my *prārabdha karma.*" That is why Sri Ramakrishna Paramahamsa says if you repeat Gita Gita Gita Gita continuously it becomes *tyāgi tyāgi tyāgi tyāgi.*

In the 68th and 69th shlokas of the Bhagavad Gita, Sri Krishna expounds the fruits of Karma Yoga and Jnāna Yoga – "Amongst My devotees, those who teach this secret knowledge perform the greatest act of love. They will come to Me without doubt. No human being performs greater service to Me than them. No one on earth is dearer to Me."

In the 66th shloka Sri Krishna promises, "Abandon all kinds of Dharma and simply surrender unto Me. I shall liberate you from all sinful reactions; do not fear."

This may appear like a paradox to us. Just now Sri Krishna said that a *tyāgi* continues to fulfill all his dharmic duties. Now why is he advising Arjuna to drop his duties and run away from the battle? If we look at this carefully we see that by *dharma*, Sri Krishna refers to doer-ship and enjoyer-ship of action. Arjuna is a *kshatriya*. He has to protect Dharma. He cannot become a monk, but he can drop the feeling, "I am the doer of this action. Therefore, I am eligible to enjoy its fruits." Then even while performing an action he is no longer the *karta* and *bhokta* – doer and enjoyer. This is true surrender. When you understand, "*nāham karta, harireva karta* – I am not the doer. God is the doer," you are absolutely free.

Sri Krishna tells Arjuna, "Don't grieve, Arjuna. Fight the war as a non-doer. Then the fruits of your action will no longer bind you. Everything that you do is an offering to God. When you drop doer-ship, the Lord operates through you." That is the summary of the Bhagavad Gita.

Sanjaya who is describing the dialogue between Sri Krishna and Arjuna to King Dhritarashtra, now tells us the *phalashruti* or merit we get by listening to the Bhagavad Gita. This is in the 78th shloka.

Wherever Sri Krishna, the Lord of Yoga and Arjuna, the supreme archer are present - infinite abundance, victory, prosperity, and righteousness always prevail. Of this, I am certain.

yatra yogeśhvaraḥ kṛishṇo
yatra pārtho dhanur-dharaḥ I
tatra srir vijayo bhūtir
dhruvā nītir matir mama II 18.78 II

In this shloka Sri Krishna represents the Bhagavad Gita, and Arjuna represents seekers like all of us. When we implement the teachings of the Gita in our lives, we are successful in the transactional world and realize our true nature. This is the summary of the 18th Chapter.

****

Shloka 42

Peacefulness, self-control, austerity, purity, tolerance, honesty, wisdom, knowledge, and religiousness - these are the qualities by which the brāhmaṇas work

śhaucham kṣhāntir ārjavam eva cha
jnānam vijnānam āstikyam
brahma-karma svabhāva-jam

śhama means peacefulness, *dama* means control over sense organs, *tapaḥ* means meditation or penance, *śhaucha* means purity, *jnāna* means knowledge, *vijnāna* means experienced knowledge, *ārjavam* means uprightness.

These are the qualities of a *brāhmaṇa*.

Someone is not called as *brāhmaṇa* just by birth. A *brāhmaṇa* is one who has certain specific qualities within him. These are some of the qualities a *brāhmaṇa* should possess. What are they?

Control of mind or **shama**: 'Shama' means restraint on the mind. The senses are external. What is the control of those senses? The mind. Who is the master of the senses? The mind. One must know to calm that mind which runs behind sense objects. But once it is trained to focus inwards, it calms down and can be controlled. This is shama.

Self-control or **dama**: Control over the sense organs. Most get excited by seeing things of the external world and run after them saying I want this and I want that - because they are attractive. A real brāhmaṇa has control over sense organs. He is moderate in indulgence with external objects.

Austerity or **tapas**: There are some different types of tapas that we can perform. For example, fasting is a kind of tapas or doing yoga is another kind. These are done to control or to develop self-control or master over the Self.

Purity or **śhauchaṁ**: When we say purity, we should consider both external purity and internal purity. Purity in thought, deed and action are some of the qualities of a brāhmaṇa.

Forbearance or **kṣhānti**: There are many occasions when some people get offended and not be able to forget those offenses for lifetime. A brāhmaṇa is one who will just forgive and forget such things and moves on in life. Why does he forgive? Because if he knows that if he does not, that hurt will continue to live in memory and will constantly disturb him. Instead of that, just forgive, forget and go ahead in life. This is the policy of a *brāhmaṇa*.

Uprightness or **ārjavam**: He is very upright in all his dealings and that makes him fearless. Whenever there is a higher goal that needs to be achieved, there is a higher purpose in life. Such a person is not afraid to call off the lower needs. He says this is the higher purpose that is to be achieved. This is called uprightness.

Knowledge and wisdom or **jnānaṁ vijnānam:** Knowledge here means all kinds of knowledge about the manifest world - what is the world, how does it operate? Knowledge about the various aspects of matter like the *tattva*, what we call as different levels of manifestation of matter, knowledge about the Self - the body, mind, intellect complex and Consciousness. A *brāhmaṇa* is clear about the world, himself and also about the God within him. This is knowledge, but theoretical knowledge. *vijnāna* means experiential knowledge. He knows not only theoretical knowledge but he also has experience of that. It is not just an understanding but a deep insight gained through meditation and inner experience.

Faith or **shraddha**: To achieve anything in life you need faith. One should have deep faith in a higher life, deep faith in God. Faith should not a blind one but with a clear understanding.

These are the hallmark characteristics of a *brāhmaṇa*, the one who is aspiring for higher consciousness.

shamo damas tapaḥ shaucham
kṣhāntir ārjavam eva cha I
jnānam vijnānam āstikyam
brahma-karma svabhāva-jam II 18.42 II

****

Shloka 54

One who is thus transcendentally situated at once realizes the Supreme Brahman. He never laments nor desires to have anything; he is equally disposed to every living entity. In that state he attains pure devotional service unto Me.

brahma-bhūtaḥ prasannātmā
na shochati na kāṅkṣhati
samaḥ sarveṣhu bhūteṣhu
mad-bhaktim labhate parām
In this shloka, God speaks about the qualities of one who has understood the essence of the scriptures,

but has not realized, he is still practicing. The scriptures say that you are Brahman – 'That you are' or *tat tvam asi*. A *brahma-bhūta* might have read and understood this very well. He can also be practicing this, but he need not have realized Brahman. Such a person is called *brahma-bhūta* - one who is practicing brahmic consciousness of the supreme reality.

prasannātmā – such a person's mind is always calm. *na śhochati na kāṅkṣhati* – many things cause disturbance to mind in life. But the *brahma-bhūta* doesn't think about them or he doesn't go after them. He has no desire for materialistic things. Not because he has realized Brahman but because he has understood through the study of scriptures and has listened to the scriptural talks. So, the attraction and repulsion of things in the world doesn't affect him intensely. But it may affect him mildly and because of his understanding of the scriptures, he will be able to overcome them easily and quickly.

samaḥ sarveṣhu bhūteṣhu – such a person is able to see all living beings with equanimity because he understands that all living beings have the presence of divinity in them. He lives with an understanding that all living beings are divine in nature.

madh-bhaktiṁ labhate parām – such a person will be immersed in supreme devotion to God. With such an outlook to life he will elevate himself and will reach higher states in consciousness. In such a state he will attain the supreme devotional service to God.

brahma-bhūtaḥ prasannātmā
na śhochati na kāṅkṣhati I
samaḥ sarveṣhu bhūteṣhu
mad-bhaktiṁ labhate parām II 18.54 II

****

Shloka 55

Only by loving devotion to Me does one come to know who I am in Truth. Then, having come to know Me, My devotee enters into full consciousness of Me.

So such a devotee, who has qualities which are outlined in the slokas, is constantly focused on the Lord.

By constantly thinking of the Lord and meditating on the Lord, he will know more and more. This is true in our life also. So, if we have interest in any subject, let us say, somebody is interested in the stock market. Because he is interested, constantly he thinks about

71

that and studies more about that and learns more and more. He is involved more and more in the stock market and he will become an expert in it. Same thing happens to a devotee. He constantly thinks about the Lord. Because he constantly thinks about the Lord he understands the quality of the Lord and understands the Lord in essence in reality and he understands that the Lord is none other than his own inner self. By knowing this ultimately he will attain Lord himself. He becomes one with the Lord.

bhaktyā mām abhijānāti
yāvān yaśh chāsmi tattvataḥ I
tato māṁ tattvato jñātvā
viśhate tad-anantaram II 18.55 II

****

Shloka 58

If you always remember Me, by My grace you shall overcome all obstacles and difficulties. But if, due to pride, you do not listen to My advice, you will perish

God gives assurance to the devotee that if you have your mind fixed on me, then you will cross over all the difficulties in life with My grace. Then there can be no obstacles for you. There could be road humps but not roadblocks. But if you don't listen to me due to ego or pride, then you will lose yourself or perish. So, does it mean God gives special attention to the devotee? Grace is always present for everybody but the devotee is able to receive it. But because of his egoistic nature, if he ignores that grace, he will be in trouble.

mach-chittaḥ sarva-durgāṇi
mat-prasādāt tariṣhyasi I
atha chet tvam ahankārān
na śhroṣhyasi vinaṅkṣhyasi II 18.58 II

****

Shloka 61

The Supreme Lord dwells in the hearts of all living beings, O Arjuna. According to their karmas, He directs the wanderings of the souls, who are seated on a machine made of material energy

īśhvaraḥ – God, where is his abode? He is in the heart of all living beings. God doesn't sit somewhere in heaven and rule the world. He's living in the heart of all living beings. Without knowing the fact that God is inside their heart, all living beings are operating as if they are independent doers.

How does God direct the 'wandering of souls' by being seated in the heart of all beings? Just like how simple machines like a fan or a tube light operate with electricity. Similarly, all living beings – the body, mind, intellect is nothing but a machine. At best you can say a biological machine or a biological robot. But the one who operates that biological machine is 'Consciousness'. One who gives energy to that biological machine is God. But once they get energy, they don't understand that God is seated inside and operating from inside. Instead, they think they are acting independently by themselves. They are deluded by the power of *maya* and they are ignorant of the presence and power of God who is seated in their heart. They think God is somewhere else and search for him.

īshvaraḥ sarva-bhūtānāṁ
hṛid-deśhe 'rjuna tiṣhṭhati I
bhrāmayan sarva-bhūtāni
yantrārūḍhāni māyayā II 18.61 II

****

Shloka 65

Always think of Me and become My devotee. Worship Me and offer your homage unto Me. Thus, you will come to Me without fail. I promise you this because you are My very dear friend.

man-manā bhava - keep your mind in me, *mad-bhakto* - become my devotee; *mad-yājī* - worship me, *māṁ namaskuru* - pray to me. Then you'll attain me. This is my assurance for you. Because you are very close to me.

Here, Bhagavān says the essence of Karma Yoga. So, when you do Karma Yoga you have to focus your mind on God. You should become a devotee and then worship God. Here he speaks about devotional service. By doing devotional service one's mind becomes pure. This is called *nishkāma karma*. It is an activity without any desire for 'self-gratification'.

All activities should be devoted to God. By doing such activities you'll purify yourself. By purifying yourself you'll become one with God. Because such a devotee is very close to God. As he's constantly thinking of God and offering all the fruits of action to God, he is close to God. Because he's close to God, he'll attain God only.

man-manā bhava mad-bhakto
mad-yājī māṁ namaskuru I
mām evaiṣhyasi satyaṁ te
pratijāne priyo 'si me II 18.65 II

****

Shloka 66

Abandon all varieties of religion and simply surrender unto Me. I shall deliver you from all sinful reactions. Do not fear

Sri Ramanujacharya considers this as the most important shloka in the Bhagavad Gita. It speaks about surrender or *sharanāgati* or *prapatti*.

sarva-dharmān parityajya – drop all *dharma*, *mām ekaṁ śharaṇaṁ vraja* – surrender unto me, *ahaṁ tvāṁ sarva-pāpebhyo mokshayiṣhyāmi mā śhuchaḥ* - I'll liberate you; I will free you from all the sins. Don't worry. This is said by Bhagavān Sri Krishna.

The concept of Dharma goes like this. Fire, for example, has both 'burning' and 'smoke' as its properties. If the nature of fire as in 'burning' is removed, then fire can no more be called as fire. The fire also gives 'smoke'. The 'burning' is the essential nature of the fire whereas 'smoke' is not the essential nature of fire. If you remove non-essential nature from fire, the fire still remains. To understand fire, the non-essential nature which is the 'smoke' should be removed.

Similarly, what is the essential nature of a human being? A human being has body, mind and intellect and consciousness. With these he performs certain roles in the world. He performs as a ruler, as an administrator, as a teacher, as a worker. So, he plays different roles. And each role has certain responsibilities and duties to be performed. So, these are all classified under as generally as Dharma.

For example, the Dharma of a *kshatriya* or a ruler is to take care of the weaker sections in the society, to protect them. That's called *kshatriya dharma*. If he doesn't do that, then that means he is not performing his Dharma.

Then there is another type of Dharma which is harma of the body (a male body or a female body), the thoughts, mind, feelings. All these things are the nature of a body. From the thoughts arises vāsanas (impressions). Depending on the type of thoughts that arise; like *sattvic* or *rājasic* or *tāmasic*, respective *vāsanas* will arise. And hence one will perform actions according to the *vāsanas*.

sarva-dharmān parityajya - Now God says surrender all the Dharma unto me. Which actually means, dropping the concept that I'm the body, I'm the mind, I'm the intellect. Drop the ego – identification with the body. All these identifications are your non-essential nature. What will happen when you drop all these identifications? What remains in you after dropping the non essential is only the essential nature. And that essential nature of you is divine. Otherwise, you're identified with the material nature - the body-mind-intellect.

Realizing that I'm not the body, I'm not the mind, I'm not the intellect, I'm Pure Consciousness, you'll become free from all Dharmas. When you realize that you are one with God in essence, you are pure consciousness, impure *vāsanas* will drop and pure *vāsanas* will come up. Gradually all *vāsanas* get exhausted and you will attain God.

So, this is the meaning of *sarva-dharman parityajya mam ekam saranam vraja*. Being one with God is your essential dharma.

sarva-dharmān parityajya
mām ekaṁ śharaṇaṁ vraja I
ahaṁ tvāṁ sarva-pāpebhyo
mokshayiṣhyāmi mā śhuchaḥ II 18.66 II

Shloka 68, 69

Amongst My devotees, those who teach this most confidential knowledge perform the greatest act of love. They will come to Me, without doubt (BG 18.68)

No human being does more loving service to Me than they; nor shall there ever be anyone on this earth more dear to Me (BG 18.69)

Every recommendation of any spiritual practice should be followed by the *phala shruti* - spelling out the importance and benefits of doing it. So what is the importance of studying Bhagavad Gita? Sri Krishna tells about the *phala shruti* in these verses.

The whole of Bhagavad Gita consists of 18 chapters and has the essential message of *tat tvam asi*, 'That Thou Are', you are one with God. This has been outlined by the Lord in 18 chapters. Can this message be given to any and everybody? No, it can be given to only those who are eligible to receive this message. It is like anything else in life. Medical science is very important. Now, can you teach medical science to everybody? Somebody has to become eligible for that, somebody has to be interested in that. We can't teach medical science to all. It's the same with engineering, physics, chemistry or art. They can be taught only to someone who is interested, who is committed.

Similarly the Bhagavad Gita can be taught to those who are interested, committed, who have the qualities for studying it. One who teaches this shastra, this scripture Bhagavad Gita to people who are interested, is a teacher of Bhagavad Gita. Such a person is very close to the Lord, because he understands the message of Bhagavān, he carries the message of Bhagavān and he lives the message of Bhagavān. One who understands the message of Bhagavān, imbibes the messages in his life and delivers the message to others is very, very close to the Lord. He is the *parama-bhakta*, a great devotee of the Lord. He is the closest to God. Such a person will attain God only because he has understood the message of God. There is none else on earth close to the Lord as much as such a devotee. The Lord gives a very special status to such a person who is teaching Bhagavad Gita.

Not only that, such a person will never be born again, He says. Here the devotee might think - ok, now God may be praising me, but tomorrow if somebody else comes, He may say 'I like you better'! The current situation is ok. But in future He may change this policy. What then? So the Lord clarifies, in future too such a person will be closest to Me. Now and forever, nobody is closer to Me other than one who teaches Bhagavad Gita. This is the message of God.

ya idaṁ paramaṁ guhyaṁ
mad-bhakteṣhv abhidhāsyati I
bhaktiṁ mayi parāṁ kṛitvā
mām evaiṣhyaty asanśhayaḥ II 68 II

na cha tasmān manuṣhyeṣhu
kaśhchin me priya-kṛittamaḥ I
bhavitā na cha me tasmād
anyaḥ priyataro bhuvi II 69 II

****

Shloka 78

Wherever there is Sri Krishna, the Lord of all yoga, and wherever there is Arjuna, the supreme archer, there will also certainly be unending opulence, victory, prosperity, and righteousness. Of this, I am certain

This is the shloka of Sanjaya, Sanjaya who is actually reporting to Dhritarashtra regarding events happening in the Kurukshetra war with his remote vision which is granted by *Sri Vedavyasa*. Sanjaya was the fortunate one who was able to listen to the Bhagavad Gita, hear Bhagavad Gita from the lips of Sri Krishna, and also see His *vishwaroopa*. After reporting the entire Bhagavad Gita, he tells Dhritarashtra that wherever there is Krishna, *yatra yogeśhvaraḥ kṛiṣhṇah,* Krishna is the *yogeshwara,* and *yatra pārtho dhanur-dharaḥ,* where there is Arjuna, there is victory. This is the meaning of the shloka.

When I say Krishna, Sri Krishna means the Lord and Arjuna is the disciple. The Lord and the disciple. The Lord is Sri Krishna and Arjuna is the disciple. We can also take Krishna as the Guru and ourselves the disciples. Or we can take Krishna as our inner self, *Atma* and Arjuna as my *jiva,* my being. Where there is Krishna implies, where there is the message of Sri Krishna - meaning the Bhagavad Gita - and 'I' as *jiva* imbibes that message in life, then there is always victory.

What is the message of Bhagavad Gita? Message of Bhagavad Gita is Yajna, service. Message of Bhagavad Gita is Yoga, union with the higher consciousness. Different types of Yoga, Karma Yoga, Bhakti Yoga, Jnāna Yoga, Kriya Yoga to higher Consciousness. So wherever we imbibe the message of Sri Krishna in our life we will always be very successful. Because Sri Krishna is our inner Self, ātma.

Sri Krishna's message is the Bhagavad Gita. If we imbibe the message of Bhagavad Gita in our life, we will be successful. This is the message of Sanjaya. And this is also a message for Dhritarashtra. 'Look Dhritarashtra, there is Krishna and here is Arjuna. They are bound to be victorious in the war…(the war has not yet started). That's Sanjaya's message for Dhritarashtra.

yatra yogeśhvaraḥ kṛiṣhṇo
yatra pārtho dhanur-dharaḥ I
tatra Srir vijayo bhūtir
dhruvā nītir matir mama II 18.78 II

****

Conclusion

Om. Truth Is. Thus in the Upanishads of the glorious Bhagavad Gita, the science of the Eternal, the scripture of yoga, the dialogue between Sri Krishna and Arjuna ends the 18th discourse titled 'The Yoga of Liberation by Renunciation'

(om tat sat iti srimad bhagavad gitāsu, upanishatsu, brahma vidyāyam yogashāstre, sri-krishna-arjuna samvāde moksha sanyāsa yogo nāma asthadasho-adhyāyaha)

This is the concluding statement of Bhagavad Gita, concluding statement of 18th Chapter. 18th Chapter is called Moksha Sanyāsa Yoga. *moksha* means liberation. Liberation can happen through *sanyāsa*. sanyāsa means renunciation. Renunciation of what? Renunciation of I, me, and mine - *ahankāra* and *mamakāra*.

I am not the body, I am not the mind, I am not the intellect. I am Pure Consciousness. This is called renunciation. This will lead to *moksha*.

Bhagavad Gita is a discussion between Sri Krishna and Arjuna (master and disciple). The essence of Bhagavad Gita is a Brahmavidya and Yogashastra.

Brahmavidya means to realize 'Who Am I?'

I am not the body, mind, and intellect. I am pure consciousness. Knowledge of the Self is called Brahmavidya.

Yogashastra means how do I apply it in life, how do I deal with society?

ātmano mokshārtham jagad hitāya. ātmano mokshārtham is Brahmavidya. *jagad hita* is achieved when we live a life of *yajna, dāna, tapas*. How to live in that way is Yogashastra. Bhagavad Gita is thus a teaching of Brahmavidya as well as Yogashastra.

This is the concluding statement of the 18th chapter.

Om Sadguru Devaya Namaha

PURCHASE DETAILS

(Scan QR codes to visit these links)

Book Purchase: https://notionpress.com/author/592662

CONTACT DETAILS

(Scan QR codes to visit these links)

Website: www.lightoftheself.org

Programs from Light of the SELF Foundation

1. **Atma Darshana** - Journey of Self discovery

2. **Jnāna Jyothi** - Study Advaita Vedanta

3. **Gita Jyoti** - Study Bhagavad Gita

4. **Yuva Jyoti** - iLeader Youth Leadership Program

5. **Bhakti Jyoti** - Learn Veda Mantras and Bhajans

6. **Yoga Jyoti** - Learn Yoga

Email id : lightofself@gmail.com